Stock Market Quickstart Guide

Everything You Need To Know To Start Trading And Investing In The Stock Market

Introduction

Congratulations and welcome to *"Stock Market Quickstart Guide: Everything you need to know to start trading and investing in the stock market."* You are here because you want to learn the ropes of making money in the stock market. I intend to show you how you can do that, to the best of my ability.

Countless people have tried to make money in the stock markets ever since the idea was invented. A few have succeeded and done well beyond anyone's dreams. At the same time, most people have crashed and burned.

It is said that more than 90% of stock market participants fail at their attempts to make money. This means that 9 out of 10 people who try to make money in stocks fail. There are numerous tales of people on Wall Street who lost all their life savings and even went deep into debt, but who are still trying to "break into the game."

When will the penny ever drop?

The interesting thing is, despite this shocking statistic, many people still invest in stocks in the hopes of making some money. It is estimated that over $200 billion exchanges hands every day in the New York Stock Exchange alone. This is evidence that people haven't given up on stocks and won't do so any time soon.

The chief cause of failure in stocks is that people begin investing in the stock market without sufficient knowledge of what they are doing. In the early 1920s, even shoe-shiners were owners of stock. When the stock market eventually went burst in 1929, it led to the greatest economic fallout in American history.

People mistakenly assume that you can make "easy money" in the stock market. In my experience, this is the worst assumption you can ever make.

The best people in the game – people who make money time and again – are people who have made it their business to know everything they can about investing in stocks. In other words, they have done their homework. This is what gives them the necessary "edge" over everyone else.

You must do the same if you ever wish to follow in their footsteps. As with anything in life worthwhile, stock investing isn't a shortcut. You must perform your due diligence.

Lucky for you, this book provides you guidance on how you can do that.

My goal in this book is simple. I intend to teach you everything you need to know about making money in the stock market before you can get started. This gives you the best chance of getting started on the right foot and avoiding the disasters that have plagued other investors.

I have written this book keeping in mind that you may be a beginner – someone who has very little experience or who has never tried their hand at making money in stocks. Therefore, I cover the basics that serve as good introductions and then slowly move on to the more complex topics that are critical to success.

Also, if you are an experienced investor, I guarantee you that you will still find much in this book that is useful to you.

I recommend that you read every chapter of this book in order. Each chapter forms the foundation for the material that comes in the next one. Skipping the chapters and going into the "juicy topics" means that you will miss out on valuable knowledge along the way – knowledge that is critical to your success. There is a reason I have arranged the information in the way I have.

By the time you are done reading this book, you will no longer be in the dark on the workings of the stock market. And this will give you the confidence to invest knowing that you are among the 10% who know what they are doing.

Does that sound good enough for you? Alright, let's begin.

Table of Contents

What You Need To Know First – Stock Market 101

This first section serves as a primer on stock market investing. In it, we cover the basics that you will need to understand before you can comfortably navigate the rest of the topics concerning the stock market.

You will look at the how the stock market works, the different classifications of stocks, the different reasons why you should invest in stocks, the main difference between trading and investing as well as the different exchanges.

Without further ado, let's jump right in.

How The Stock Market Works

In discussing how the stock market works, we are going to begin by first defining what a stock is.

So what is it?

A stock is simply a financial instrument (usually in the form of a certificate) that is meant to represent an ownership stake in a company. Another name for a stock is _equity._

When you are an owner of stock belonging to a certain company, you have a claim on the assets as well as the earnings of the business. Normally, your ownership is always expressed as a percentage of the outstanding shares. For instance, if you own 10,000 shares in a company that has 1,000,000 outstanding shares, then you are said to own a 10% stake in that company.

So the next question you may have is, "How do companies issue stocks and why?"

How And Why Companies Issue Stocks

The main reason why companies issue stocks to the public is simple – to raise capital for expansion.

Let me explain.

The thing is; most companies that currently trade on the stock exchange started out as private companies. When a company is operating as private, it typically has access to limited sources of capital. Most of the time, funding may come from the entrepreneur's savings, donations from family and friends or from bank loans.

When a company is just starting out, these sources of capital seem to work just fine. Afterwards, if the company operates profitably and attains growth, it may manage to attract funding from angel investors, private equity, sovereign wealth funds, as well as venture capitalists.

When a company has grown past this point, and still wishes to expand its operations -for instance operating globally – it will need additional funding. At this point, the company may either choose to obtain a bank loan, or raise funds from the public (equity financing).

Equity financing is always the best choice for most companies since it is the cheapest way of sourcing funds. Bank loans often require a business to pledge its assets as collateral, which it may not have. They also carry interests which may negatively impact on the performance of the business especially in its early stages of operation.

At this point, the owner of the company along with other investors in the company may decide to reach out to major banks that can serve as underwriters of an ***Initial Public Offering (or IPO).*** Underwriting is the process of determining the value of a company, creating shares, and selling those shares to the public so that funds can be raised.

Examples of banks that underwrite IPOs include:

- Credit Suisse

- Merrill Lynch

- Goldman Sachs

- J.P Morgan

- Citi Bank

- Morgan Stanley, among others

After the underwriters have marketed the IPO to potential investors, and the SEC has done a background check on the company considering the IPO, a date for selling shares to the public is set. The investors then start bidding on the price of the stock in the primary market.

Individual investors mostly don't get involved at this point since "big money" is always thrown at the stock making it highly volatile; only hedge funds, mutual funds, pension funds, big banks, wealthy individuals and the like always get involved at this point. They become the initial buyers of the stock. This money is always handed over to the company.

If the IPO is successful, the price is always driven up to certain value before it stabilizes. This is the point where the investors in the IPO (including the underwriter) always cash in on their investment. After stabilizing, the stock is then sold in the *aftermarket (or the secondary market)* - the one that mostly constitutes of small investors like you and me.

This is also the time the company is listed on an exchange such as the New York Stock Exchange.

The Stock Market

The stock market simply refers to the secondary market where buyers and sellers of stock in publicly traded companies conduct business.

Keep in mind that the company issuing shares does not conduct business in the stock market. The stock market simply consists owners of stock and their potential buyers.

If a company decides to issue more shares or conduct a stock buyback, it can. However, such deals are occasional and mostly happen in the primary market which is not always open to the public.

Business in the stock market is always conducted in an auction fashion. The seller of a stock usually provides an offer (or asking price). This is the lowest price that he or she is willing to accept in order to sell. The buyer then provides the bid. This is the highest price that he or she is willing to accept in order to buy. When the two parties agree on a price, a transaction takes place.

Transactions like these usually happen in an exchange, such as the New York Stock Exchange. A broker usually sits between the buyer side and the selling side to facilitate the exchange and ensure a fair market. They usually pocket a commission on the transactions executed.

In the past, transactions would take place in an exchange through a method called _open outcry_. A broker on a floor would shout the price of a stock and then start taking bids from the other traders on the pit. The trader who offers the best terms first gets the deal.

Today, that process is mostly digitized through computers. Most people who participate in the stock trade online from home or at the office, as it is cheaper, more convenient, and faster.

However, you will still find many traders even today, conducting business in the pit using the open outcry method since they deem it the most efficient way to trade large blocks of securities such as those owned by large market participants like banks and corporations.

For instance, you may find a trader representing a company selling as much as $200 million worth of stock at a clip on the floor. Brokers usually find it difficult to execute such transactions electronically at the best price. So the open outcry method is usually the best for this purpose.

However, for ordinary individual investors like you who may want to trade perhaps $500, $1,000, or even $100,000 at a time, you can easily conduct these transactions efficiently, and cheaply online.

Now that you are well-acquainted with how the stock market works, let us look at the different stock exchanges that you should know of.

The Different Stock Exchanges

We have just seen that transactions involving buyers and sellers of stock happen at an exchange. And when it comes to that, there are three main stock exchanges here in the U.S, which you ought to be aware of.

They are:

1: The New York Stock Exchange

Unless you have been living under a rock ever since you were born, you probably already know about this one. It was founded in the year 1792 and is located at 11 Wall Street in Manhattan, New York City.

It rose to stardom after the United States won the First World War. The economy was so strong back then and people became very optimistic about the future. People began snapping up stocks belonging to various household names that were listed in the New York Stock Exchange.

Today, it has earned its name as world's largest and most famous stock exchange. It is home to the largest corporations in the world such as U.S Steel, General Motors, Exxon Mobil, and others. Most reputable companies in the world that plan on going public prefer to be listed at this exchange, more than anywhere else.

As of 2018, it was estimated that the market capitalization of companies listed in this exchange exceeded $30 trillion. By the way, market capitalization is simply a way of referring to the total monetary value of a company's outstanding shares.

If company A has 100 million outstanding shares, and the current market value of the stock is at $20 per share, then you would simply need to multiply the two to get the market capitalization of that particular company.

In our case, that is:

$$\$20 \quad x \quad 100{,}000{,}000 \quad = \quad 2{,}000{,}000{,}000$$

Therefore, the market capitalization of company A is $2 billion.

The companies listed in the New York Stock Exchange have to be approved by the SEC and can never be listed at any other exchange.

2: Nasdaq

This is the second most popular stock exchange in the world and was started in the year 1971. It is located at 165 Broadway, New York and the total market capitalization of companies listed in this exchange exceeds $10 trillion.

The name is actually an acronym for the National Association of Securities Dealers Automated Quotations – the company that still owns it.

It holds its reputation as the first electronic stock exchange ever, an idea that was later adopted by other exchanges in the world. This brought transparency in prices as well as ease of operation in the stock market unlike ever before. The low brokerage fees plus the ease of buying and selling stock online that you enjoy today is an idea that was first pioneered by the founders of NASDQ.

In the beginning, most of the companies you could find listed in the NASDQ exchange were primarily tech stocks. Today, here is where you will find companies such as Amazon, Oracle, Dell, Google, Microsoft, Apple, and the like listed.

3: American Stock Exchange

Lastly, we talk about the American Stock Exchange or (AMEX).

This exchange was established in the year 1911 by traders who wanted to operate independently on the street. It became the main competitor of the New York Stock Exchange up until NASDAQ took that position.

The American Stock exchange primarily focuses on small-cap and mid-cap companies. These are companies whose market capitalizations range from between $250 million to $10 billion. We will talk about them later on.

Also, the American Stock Exchange is where many complex financial instruments such as derivatives, mortgage-backed securities, collateralized debt obligations, options and exchange traded funds (or ETFs) are traded. Most of the trading conducted here is also electronic.

This concludes our discussion of Stock exchanges. There are many others such as the Chicago Stock Exchange, the National

Stock Exchange, The Miami Stock Exchange, and others, but knowing about them is nearly as important as the ones we have just discussed.

Let us now look at the different stock classifications.

Stock Classifications

There are different categories of stock. Depending on your situation and your objective behind your investment, you may prefer to go for certain types of stock more than others. Let us look at what those categories are:

i)   *Income stocks*

The first category of stocks is known as income stocks. These are stocks that are issued by companies that are large, stable and have stood the test of time.

Companies that qualify as income stocks are usually leaders in their respective sectors; think Exxon Mobil, Royal Dutch Shell, Microsoft, General Motors and the like.

They are labeled income stocks because investors primarily invest in them if they wish to get regular incomes from their investment. This income usually comes in the form of dividend payments.

These companies can afford to pay dividends because they have dominated their industries and therefore have little room for growth. Therefore, the management always deems it better to give back the profits to the investors instead of ploughing them back into the company.

Since these companies have stabilized and have a great track record, they are always considered the least risky. Therefore, these stocks are good for you if you consider yourself to be more conservative than most investors are, and wish to get a steady income from your investment despite the movement of the stock price.

ii)   *Value stocks*

Next, we have value stocks. The definition of a value stock is a stock that trades at a lower price than its intrinsic value. In other words, this is a company whose stock is simply undervalued. A common characteristic is that these companies are valued at a lower price than most other companies in their sectors.

Value stocks are mostly preferred by value investors – people who buy a company's stock at a bottom-dollar price simply because they believe that in the future, the price will skyrocket. They like to think of it as purchasing a valuable stock at a bargain. Warren Buffet is one good example of such an investor.

There are many reasons why a company's stock may be undervalued.

The most common reasons include:

- The company is new and most people haven't made up their mind about it.

- The industry is going through a bit of trouble but is likely to rebound

- The stock doesn't fit the criteria for most investments but is likely to, in the future.

These stocks may be good for you especially if you don't consider yourself good at speculation – which is highly competitive. It is also a good investment for you if you are young since most value stocks take a significant amount of time before they eventually come around and realize their potential.

iii) Growth stocks

Another class of stock is growth stocks. These are stocks belonging to companies that are expected to grow at a much faster rate than the stock market in general.

The reason why they are expected to do this is because most of their profits (if not all) are usually re-invested in the business. For this reason, many growth stocks do not pay dividends. Most of their investors expect to earn a return on their investment via capital gains – when the value of the stock goes up.

Since these companies pay virtually no dividends at all, they are always considered to have a higher risk profile than value stocks. They are preferred by people who consider themselves to be "risk takers".

If you are one of them, these are the right stocks for you.

Most growth stocks belong to sectors such as technology, biotech and consumer products.

iv) Speculative stocks

Speculative stocks are a unique class of stocks mainly issued by startups.

A common feature of startups is that most of the time, they are controversial. Most are highly innovative, and have ventured into untapped markets, which are mostly foreign and/or new. Many show great potential for growth but uncertainty still lurks in the air for most investors.

For this reason, many of these stocks are highly volatile and therefore very risky. As a matter of fact, most of these stocks were responsible for the bust of the dot-com bubble.

The internet had started becoming very popular back then and new companies founded on the internet were assumed to have great potential. It was a good time for young tech companies to go public.

Underwriters on Wall Street were eager to exploit this situation. So they exploited companies like Netscape – companies that were taken public even though the business ideas behind them were never solid.

They cleverly marketed them, took them public, pumped up the stock prices (cashing in big in the process), dumped them and left them for dead.

You can consider these stocks if your goal is to speculate.

v)   *Penny stocks*

By definition, these are stocks whose value is at $5 or less.

The companies that make up penny stocks are frequently small companies. Some of them are traded in the New York

Stock Exchange but most are traded in the (Over-The-Counter) market or (OTC as it is often called).

The OTC is an exchange where companies that have failed to meet minimum requirements to be listed in the NYSE, NASDAQ or AMEX are traded.

They are bought and sold via an electronic bulletin board or privately owned pink sheets.

Since not many investors flock the OTC, many of these stocks often lack liquidity. Liquidity simply means the ability to get in and out of a market whenever you wish because there is always a ready buyer or seller at any given time. A lack of liquidity means that prices thrash around frequently and often in a very unpredictable manner. Therefore, trading penny stocks is often a very risky venture.

However, believe or not, despite all this negative hype, some people have actually found great success in this strange market. Timothy Sykes became a millionaire at age 21 back in 2002 trading penny stocks, and has done well for many years since then. He even featured in the prime-time hit docuseries *"Wall Street Warriors"*. To this day, he still trades penny stocks and has a net worth of $15 million.

vi)   Defensive stocks

Lastly, we have defensive stocks. These are stocks that are usually considered the "perfect safety-nets" during periods of an economic crisis. This is because their businesses are always considered recession-proof.

During a period of an economic downturn- such as the one we witnessed during the 2008 housing crisis - the prices of these stocks always seem to go up. This is because demand for their products and services becomes greater even as the economic situation gets worse.

Stocks that belong to this special category come from sectors such as healthcare, foodstuff, fuel, and utilities. You can keep these stocks as an insurance policy or a plan B that prevents you from going bankrupt, should such unfortunate events ever occur.

This is where we conclude our discussion of the various categories of stocks. Next, we will look at a few important benefits you can get from becoming an investor in stocks.

Why Invest In Stocks

Investing in stocks has its perks. It is important that you know about them so that you can learn to appreciate the opportunity.

Let us look at what those benefits are:

1) Getting started is easy

Unlike most ventures, getting started investing in the stock market is really easy. It's cheap too.

After mastering the basics of investing in the stock market – which is what you will learn in this book – you will only need to save up a few dollars, open a brokerage account and start buying shares. Even a few hundred dollars will get you far, as long as you keep adding to that investment.

If you are a busy person who has always wanted to invest, you can't imagine anything being better than this. You just do a little bit of research on good candidates to invest in, you put your money in them and then you just check on them for no more than 5 minutes every day.

Very few businesses allow you to operate with that much ease and flexibility. Most businesses require massive capital, endless paperwork, rental costs, paying for manpower and a lot of other endless details that can make your head spin.

2) You stay ahead of inflation

Inflation is always a real problem when it comes to money. It is estimated that inflation eats away at the value of your money at an average of 4% every year.

This is one of the reasons why being too conservative or risk averse when it comes to money is often a serious problem. If you choose to save instead of investing, I can guarantee that you will lose big time.

To illustrate, let us look at some of the best annual interest rates you could ever find on savings accounts today:

- Citibank   -   2.36%

- Vio Bank   -   2.52%

- Goldman Sacchs   -   2.15%

- HSBC direct   -   2.20%

- American Express -   2.10%

As you can see, you would be lucky to get a savings account that earns enough interest to beat inflation, as there isn't one according to this list.

It is much better to put your money in stocks than to have it in a bank since historically, stocks have been known to outperform the inflation rate. According to CNN Money stocks have always performed at an average annualized rate of 10% per year.

This means that even without sophisticated market knowledge, merely putting your money in stocks puts you in the driver's seat when it comes to beating inflation. Arm yourself with a little bit of market skill and you will get returns that would even make a professional banker lose their sleep.

3) High liquidity

Liquidity is an important factor when it comes to investing, and this is one of the best reasons why you may choose to go into stocks.

The reality is, there are many other good investment vehicles out there. Real estate is one good example. The problem with real estate is that it suffers from a lack of sufficient liquidity.

If you buy a piece of property today that ends up appreciating in value in the next five years, exiting that investment isn't always an easy feat as one might imagine. Ready buyers are not always within reach. You may have to spend money on marketing so as to attract potential buyers.

If marketing isn't your cup of tea, you may have to involve professional real estate brokers, who usually charge an awful lot for such services. Then comes the paperwork; closing such deals requires serious paperwork and you may even have to involve real estate attorneys to go over them. Such services come at a price.

The bottom-line is investing in real estate is a tedious and risky process. Even shopping for property requires meticulous research and prices aren't usually transparent. The possibility of getting ripped off is always real.

Comparatively, stocks are much easier to deal with. There are so many participants in stocks, such that liquidity is always guaranteed at any given time. You could purchase a company's stock in just a few seconds, and sell it after maybe an hour, or even just a few minutes. A ready market always exists.

Also, the clearing house is always required by law to guarantee the liquidity. There is no point in time - even in crazy bear markets-when you will find no buyer for your stock if you decide to sell.

4) You can profit in either direction

This is one of the biggest advantages of participating in capital markets such as stocks. You can make money whether the market falls or rises.

Most people are familiar with buying something when the price is low and selling at a much higher price. In the world of speculation it is called going long, and is the most straightforward way to make money in a bull market – a market where prices are consistently rising.

What most people do not know is that you can also do the opposite – sell when prices are high and buy back when prices are low. It is called going short and is the perfect thing to do in a bear market – a market where prices are consistently going down.

This kind of flexibility allows you to take advantage of any economic situation. You do not have to be loyal to one side. You can make money even when things are going bad for a company or the economy in general.

Most people who are not informed on matters concerning investments don't have the slightest idea about this. And this is one of the reasons why most people become poor when economic storms hit. In reality, such events are always golden opportunities for you to cash in big.

To illustrate, Jesse Livermore – one of the best investors America has ever had - went short on stocks in 1929 as the stock market was crashing and everyone was going broke. In total, he cashed in an excess of $100 million during that time alone. That was serious money back then. Adjusted for inflation, such an amount would be the equivalent of approximately $1.1 billion.

That was the same thing that happened in in the stock market crash of 1987. Paul Tudor jones went short on stocks and made over $100 million. Then there was the legendary George Soros who shorted the British pound on a massive scale in 1991 and made over £1 billion pounds – the biggest record in speculative history.

The last example of George Soros may have drifted to another type of market (currencies), but the point remains the same. You can make money even in falling financial markets.

Stories of Jesse Livermore, Paul Tudor Jones and George Soros and many others like them weren't the only ones that existed. These were public figures and that is why their stories are widely known. Many investors who weren't famous – people like you and me - made a lot of money back then as well.

There are very few ventures in this world that give you chances like these.

At this point, you are well conversant with the basics of the stock market. In the next section, we will take things further and start discussing strategies. See you there.

Different Strategies

Investing successfully over a life-time requires use of strategy. Why? Because participating in the financial markets is never a sure thing. There is inherent risk involved. Sure, you could gamble every now and then, but you can never expect to get lucky in the markets every time. You need a proven methodology that can stack the odds of success in your favor.

And that is what this section focuses on. We will discuss everything you will need to know about strategy as well as a few good ones that you can use. You will also take a small test designed to help you identify the best strategy you can apply to your stock market investment. Let's go.

Trading Vs. Investing

Let me first begin by explaining the difference these two. This is important because your approach to the stock markets will fall under these two; every strategy out there is either one that belongs to trading or investing.

Therefore, it is important that you are able to tell the difference.

What is trading?

Trading is what I have referred up to this point as speculation. It is a way of seeking short-term gains from the financial markets by attempting to predict the future movement of prices of a financial instrument such as a stock. Traders are not concerned with the intrinsic value of an asset or its long-term performance. The only concern of a trader is how he or she can make a profit from the movement of prices.

Since traders are mostly concerned with movement of prices, the classic tools used are technical analysis tools and trading systems (we will look at technical analysis later on). A trader will rely on things like charts, trend lines, moving averages and many others. These tools are built into any trading software you will get out there.

The beauty about becoming a trader or speculator is that you can make profit whether the market goes up or down; a trader can buy or go long when the market is going up and sell or go short when the market goes down.

Since traders operate with this kind of flexibility, they are thought to have access to more opportunities as compared to investors.

Based on the time a trader can hold an investment alone, traders can be put into four different categories. They are:

i)   *Position traders:* these are traders that hold positions in the market for months to even years on end.

ii)   *Swing traders:* Swing traders can hold a position in the market for weeks or even months.

iii) *Day traders:* These are traders who hold positions for no longer than a day.

iv)   *Scalpers:* Scalpers get in and out of positions within minutes and sometimes even seconds. Scalpers can execute several transactions in a typical day – sometimes even more than a hundred.

What is investing?

Investing, on the other hand, is very different.

Unlike traders, investors are more concerned with the long-term performance of an asset. If it is a company, as is the case in stocks, they will be looking to see how the company will perform in the next five years, ten years or more. They are not interested in making a profit by the end of the day, week or month.

Investors also tend to operate in only one direction – the buy side. It is rare that an investor will look to short a market. The belief of a trader is that even though a market may move up and down, if the asset is a good one, it will eventually go up. So investors tend to sit through up and downward price movements with the hopes of eventually turning a profit.

Another difference between investors and speculators is that investors tend to rely on fundamentals to perform their analysis. Technical analysis has little value to investors since they don't make their decisions based on price. They are interested in the intrinsic value. So you will find an investor paying more attention to the profit earned this quarter instead of something like prices breaking below a trend line.

It is important to note that since traders need to track prices more frequently, there is more work involved in trading. So many independent traders take up trading either as a full-time job or part time. But the job needs focus and high competence.

Investing, on the other hand, is a more passive income activity. If you are busy, you may want to choose investing since you will rarely need to stay in touch with prices every single minute, hour or day. If your plan is to exit your investment in 10 years, tracking prices the way a speculator does is a waste of time. You are better off taking a vacation or focusing on your day-job.

There you have it.

Now you know the difference between the two. Let us now take a look at how you can find good stocks to invest in using both fundamental and technical analysis.

How To Find Good Stocks To Invest In

In stock marketplace, there are both good and bad places to put your money. Your main job as someone who wants to make money in stocks is to come up with an appropriate strategy that helps you select the best opportunities that are more likely to turn a profit for you.

I say "likely" to highlight an important point.

As a stock market participant, you can never expect to make money on all your transactions. Some will make money and some won't. Nobody ever makes money 100% of the time. Not even the best of the best. A good strategy is that which helps you make more money than you lose.

That said, let us start with technical analysis.

Technical Analysis - Short Term Trading Strategies

Previously, I mentioned that technical analysis is mostly used by speculators. Investors may use it at times, but that happens in very rare occasions and for very specific reasons – such as when designing an exit strategy. I am going to give you a short introduction to technical analysis.

Technical analysis is a deep subject that could actually take up a whole book on its own, but I am guessing you have little interest in that. You are only interested in knowing what is necessary to help you get started in trading as quickly as you can. After covering the basics, I am going to show you a few simple technical trading strategies that you can use to make money in the markets.

So let's start from the beginning.

What is technical analysis really?

Technical analysis is simply a way of evaluating an investment and spotting opportunities that makes use of patterns identified from the statistical analysis of price movement. These patterns are identified using technical tools such as charts and technical indicators.

Charts

Charts are the most basic way of representing price information about a particular financial asset such as a stock. And when it comes to that, there are three main types of charts that you will need to know of as an investor or speculator. These charts are found on literally every trading software in existence.

They are:

i) *Line charts*

This is the most basic type of chart. It is used to plot the closing prices of a particular stock within a certain period of time. Since these charts only plot the closing prices, you will rarely use them because this kind of information is too limited for you to make any major trading decision. However, you may find them useful for identifying the common trend. In this case, you could say that the market is trending upwards.

ii) *Bar charts*

Then we have bar charts, with a good example being the one you can see below.

Even though this isn't the most popular chart you will find today, a good number of traders use it. Mainly, this is because it is able to plot more information about prices on the chart. As you can see from the figure above, a bar chart can plot the opening price, the closing price, the highest price for the day, and the lowest price for the day.

I talk about "the day" because as you can see the char is labeled *'Daily'*. That is the timeframe for that chart. There is a single bar appearing on the chart marking each day that passes. In this case, that is from 20th February to 13th March. You can tweak the settings to other timeframes such as 1 hour, 30 minutes, 15 minutes, 5 minutes, even 1 minute, depending on the trading software you are using.

It is important to note that trading software represent bullish bars and bearish bars differently. According to the chart above, the bullish bars are colored in black. The ones marked red are the bearish ones.

A bullish bar is one which the prices open higher than the last close. A bearish bar is one where prices open lower than the last close. This information can be valuable when designing a trading strategy.

iii) Candlestick charts

Lastly, but not the least, you have a candlestick chart.

These are the most common types of charts used by investors and traders across the investment community. They are my favorite type of chart too.

They track the same type of information as the bar charts, but represent it in a much more visually appealing way. Here is one example of a candlestick chart.

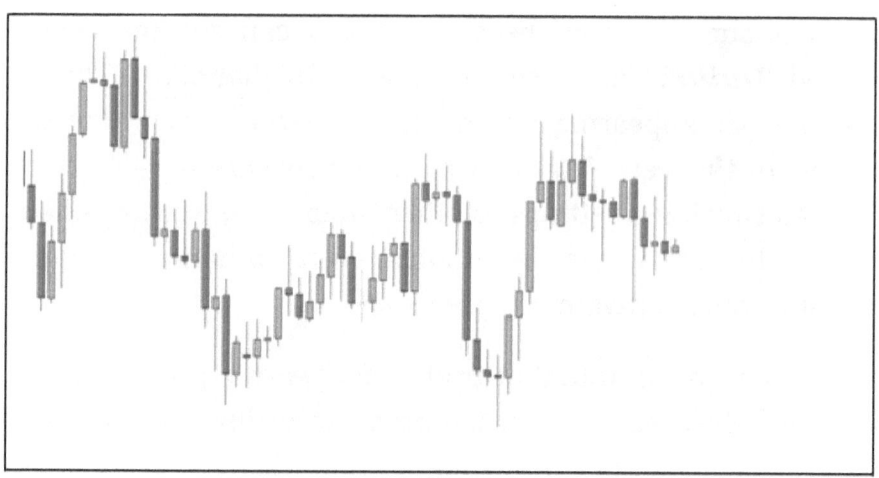

Here too, the trading software draws a clear line between bullish and bearish candlesticks. The bullish candlesticks are filled with green color while the bearish candlesticks are filled with red. In some trading software, you will find bullish candlestick looking empty while the bearish ones are filled with a solid color such as black.

The picture below shows the type of information that a candlestick represents. As you can see, there is a striking resemblance between candlesticks and bars.

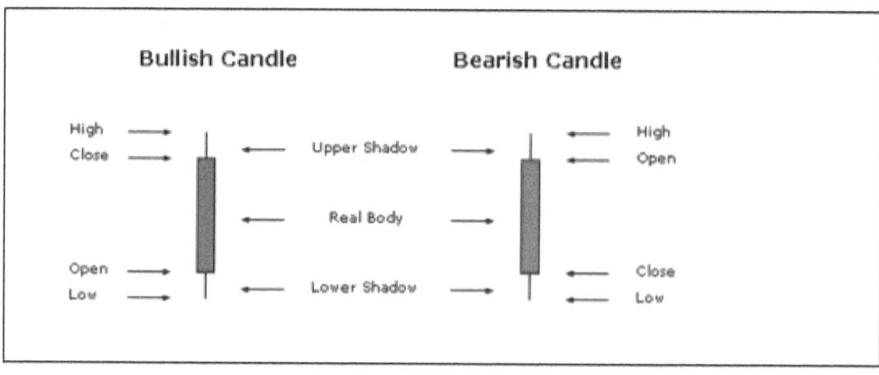

Now that we are done discussing charts, let us look at another important class of technical analysis tools – technical indicators

About Technical Indicators

Charts by themselves don't provide you with much to work with. If you intend to develop a reliable trading strategy - or system, as it is sometimes called – you will need to add technical indicators as well.

So what are technical indicators really?

They are simply tools that rely on mathematical equations and calculations and are used to evaluate price data about a particular financial instrument. In my experience, indicators mainly serve as confirmation signals in technical trading systems.

There are many indicators out there...hundreds of them...perhaps even thousands. Knowing all about them is never important. You simply need to get acquainted with a few common ones that can help you design the strategy or system that you want.

Let's look at them.

i)   Trend lines

The first indicator is a trend line. I wouldn't label it as an indicator per se, since it isn't constructed using mathematical calculations. A better term would be a charting tool.

So what is it?

A trend line is simply a line that is usually drawn across two or more points across a trading chart. It is one of the simplest and most common tools in trading, and certainly one of the most important. The goal in drawing this line is to determine the predominant trend in a particular market. As you can see from the diagram below, the trend-line has been drawn indicating that the trend is upwards. Such a trend line is always called an *"Uptrend line"*

It is important to note that trend lines are usually drawn below the wicks of the candlesticks for accuracy reasons.

ii)   Moving averages

Then we have a class of indicators called moving averages. These are indicators used to calculate the averages of the prices of a stock or other security over a certain period of time.

They are frequently used as "automated trend lines" in many trading strategies. They are automated because the computer calculates the averages for you and plots the line.

You must know that there are two types of moving averages: Simple moving average (SMA) and exponential moving average (EMA). Simple moving averages track the averages over a much longer period of time, while exponential moving averages track prices that are more recent.

When it comes to tracking the trend, EMAs are considered to be much more effective than SMAs.

For example, here is a chart showing an EMA with a period setting of 200 tracking an uptrend on the stock of General Electric.

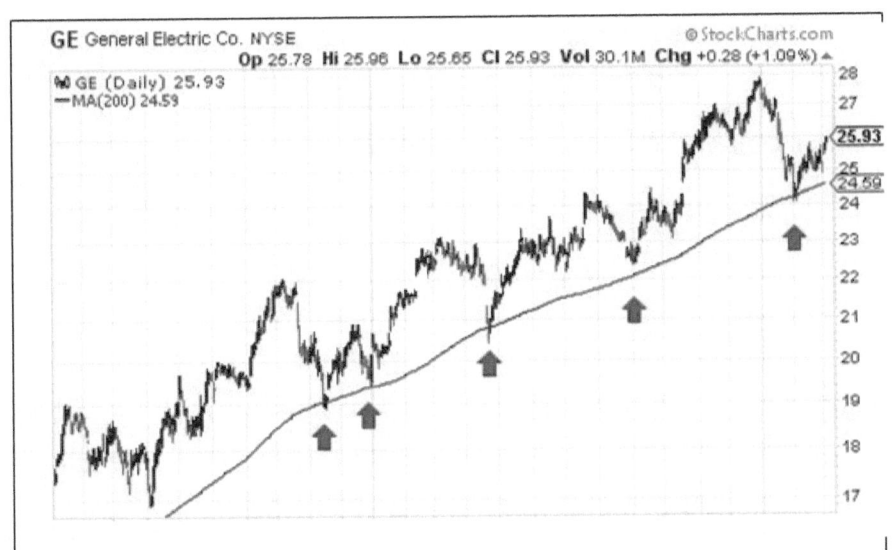

iii) *Commodity Channel Index (CCI)*

We also have an indicator called the commodity channel index.

This indicator is mostly used to track overbought or oversold conditions in the market. Such signals are especially important when trading momentum-based or range-based systems in the markets.

Using it is pretty simple; when the line in the indicator window moves above the +100 mark, you are looking at an overbought condition. On the other hand, if the line crosses below -100, you are looking at an oversold condition.

Take a look at the chart below.

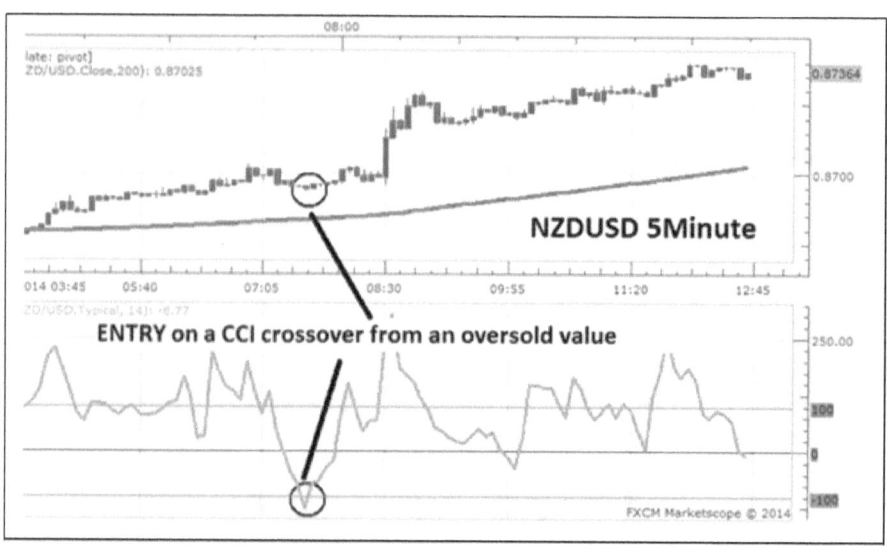

The CCI crossed above the +100 mark at about the time when the market was breaking from a tight range. This could be used as a signal to go long on a particular stock.

vii) *Relative Strength Indicator (RSI)*

Then there is the Relative Strength Indicator (or RSI).

This is an indicator that works in a similar way to the CCI. It is designed to be a momentum indicator. It is displayed as a line graph in a window and the y axis marked from 0 to 100.

To use this indicator, you need to keep your eye on two numbers 70 and 30. If the line crosses below 30, it denotes and undersold situation. But, if the line crosses above 70, it indicates an overbought situation.

Check the chart below. In this case you are looking at a sideways range-bound market. When the price gets closer to the previous high, the market reverses. This is a great shorting opportunity. The same happens when the price gets to the previous low indicating a great buying opportunity.

As you can see, the RSI is behaving accordingly.

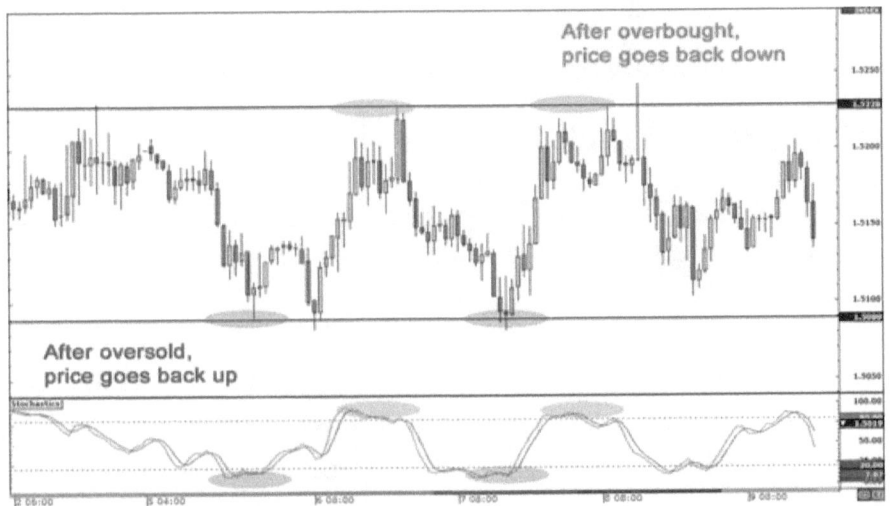

Now that you have the basics of fundamental analysis under your belt, let us look at some simple short-term trading strategies that you can apply.

Simple Short-Term Trading Strategies

You have just learnt that, in order for you to operate successfully in the financial markets, you must implement a strategy. And when it comes to that, there are countless strategies out there. Some are good and some aren't that good. Some are simple, and some are downright difficult to work with.

Teaching you a few basic but workable strategies that can quickly get you started in the markets is one of my most important goals in this book. Many people are under the impression that you need a complicated strategy to be successful – you don't. You just need to find a simple strategy that works. Then you can stick with that strategy for as long as it works.

Let us look at what some of those strategies are.

1: Trending Markets

Making money in a trending market is one of the most popular and time-tested ways of making money in the financial markets. It's also remarkably simple.

To begin, a trending market is that which prices seem to move in a certain direction with only a few retracements in the move. This direction can either be up or down. A market that is trending upwards is said to be in an Uptrend. Conversely a Downtrend describes a market that is trending downwards.

Trading An Uptrend

The basic idea in trading an uptrend is to buy into the lows (also called the pullbacks or retracements). A market can never go straight up; even the strongest trends retrace at some point.

Your goal as a trader is to buy or go long at these retracements. Then, when the movement is back on track, you stand to make a profit. Do this consistently and you stand to make quite some nice profits.

Therefore, what you need to do is first draw trend lines. A valid trend line is that which connects more than two retracements on the chart. Well, you can rely on one that connects only two, but having at least three past retracements connected by your line is better.

The expectation is that a good retracement to buy into will develop close to the trend line or above the trend line. Once you spot any of these situations, you have a green light on placing your trade.

However, refrain from trading retracements that appear below the line. When the market does this, you are supposed to assume that the market has broken the trend and is either reversing its direction or transitioning into a sideways direction.

As you can see from this other chart, when the market broke the trend line, it transitioned to a downtrend.

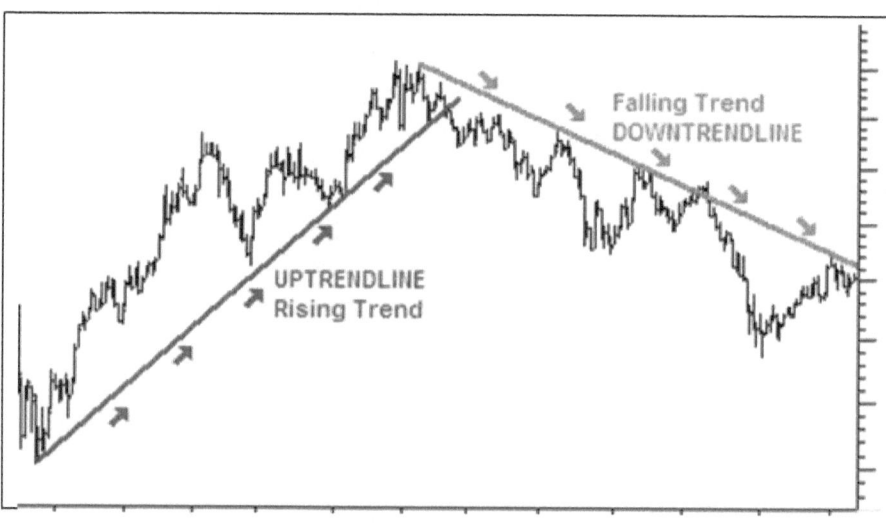

Another consideration you have to make in this strategy is the location of your stop-loss order. A stop-loss order in trading is an order that protects you from losing your all or most of your capital should the market fail to act in your favor. It does this by automatically selling and closing your position. It is the most basic form of risk management you can ever implement in your trading.

Don't forget – no matter how good your strategy is, you can never assume that any given trade will work out. The best you can do is be prepared for such a scenario and avoid losing a significant portion of your capital. This gives you the chance to take another opportunity that could work in your favor next time. Putting a stop-loss order on every trade you place is the best way of ensuring that.

So, the best location to put your stop-loss order is just below a retracement. The chart below best illustrates this point. The areas marked red are your best areas to place a stop-loss order in such a market.

As the market keeps moving in your favor, you keep on raising your stop-loss order to the next retracement so that you lock in on profits and protect your investment. This is always known as *"trailing a stop"*.

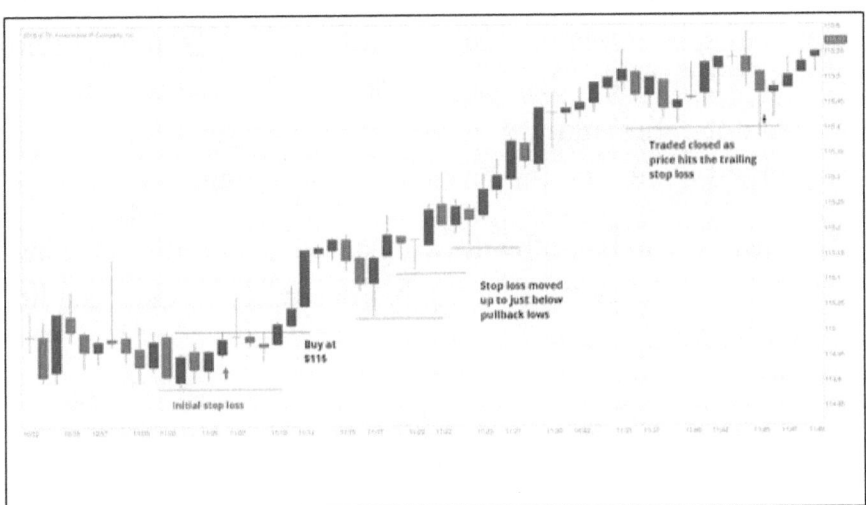

In addition to a stop-loss order, you will also need a "take-profit" order; every good trading strategy has one. This order automatically sells your investment so that you pocket a profit, should the market hit your profit target. And just like the stop-loss, you can also move this order as the market moves in your favor so that you pocket even more profit.

The best place to put your take-profit order is at a distance that is at least twice that which is between your entry price and the stop-loss order. This gives you a risk reward ratio of *1:2*. If the trend is a good one, this profit target should be hit.

Now that you know how to trade an uptrend, let's look at how you can trade a downtrend.

Trading A Downtrend

Trading a downtrend is easy. Once you know how to trade an uptrend, it's simply a matter of repeating the same concepts, just in reverse.

As you well know by now, a downtrend is a market where prices keep moving downwards with some minor retracements. The idea is to short the market at the retracements; the market never goes straight down. These retracements offer you the best chance of selling.

So, as always, you begin by drawing a downtrend line as shown by this chart. The retracements that occur at or below the line are your best entry signals.

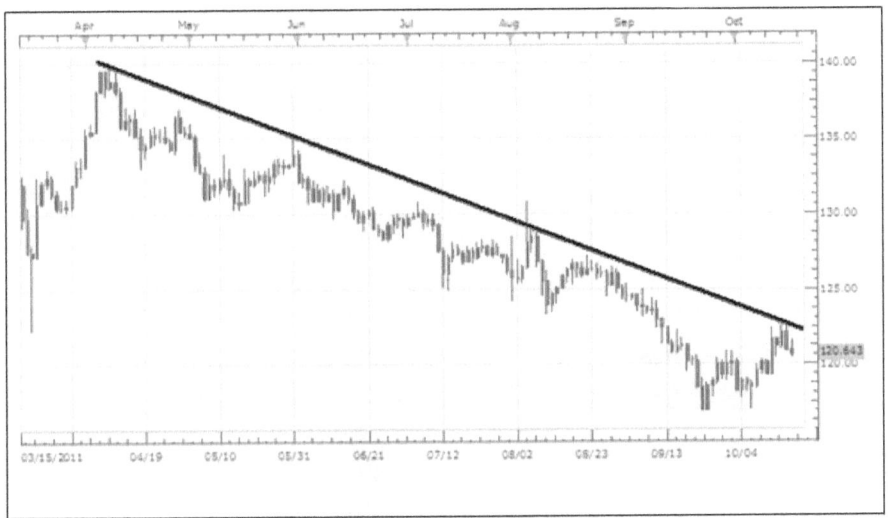

The stop-loss order needs to be placed just above the retracements and the take-profit order, at a distance twice that between the entry price and the stop-loss.

Now you know how to trade and profit from trending markets. Let's look at sideways markets.

2: Sideways Markets

The market only moves in three directions – upwards, downwards and sideways.

It is a known fact in the world of trading that the market trends only 40% of the time. The rest of the time, it moves sideways. So, knowing how to trade both trending and sideways markets gives you a significant advantage when it comes to spotting market opportunities.

There are many ways to trade sideways markets. But, for the purposes of this book, we will look at two simple strategies each targeting two main sideways market setups.

Trading A Wide-Ranging Market

The first sideways market set-up you will encounter is that of a market that seems to be stuck in a wide range. It isn't always clear to someone who isn't used to looking at charts because patterns in the market aren't always exact.

But if you focus your eyes a little bit, you should be able to spot it. In fact, training your eyes to see certain things is one of the most important skills you could ever arm yourself with.

If you are keen enough, you should be able to notice that prices are bouncing-off in both directions at some imaginary line. It's as if there is something that is preventing them from going further, once they reach a certain point. Take a look at this chart.

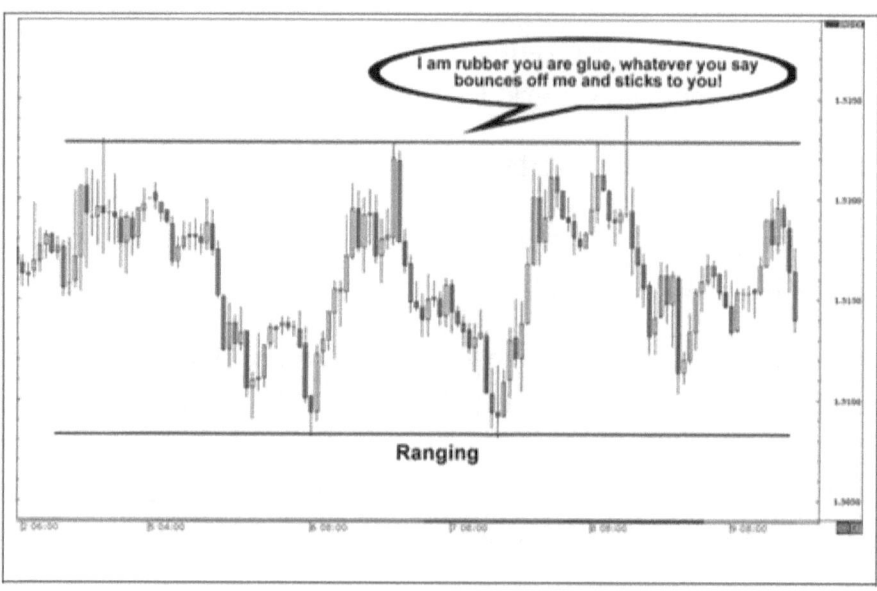

The main idea in this kind of setup is to plan on shorting the market at the highs (also called resistance) and going long at the lows (support) as illustrated in this diagram. Doing this gives you the best chance of profiting from this kind of market.

So the first thing you do is draw the horizontal lines connecting the highs and lows. These lines help you identify the main "decision levels". Then you plan your entries and exits.

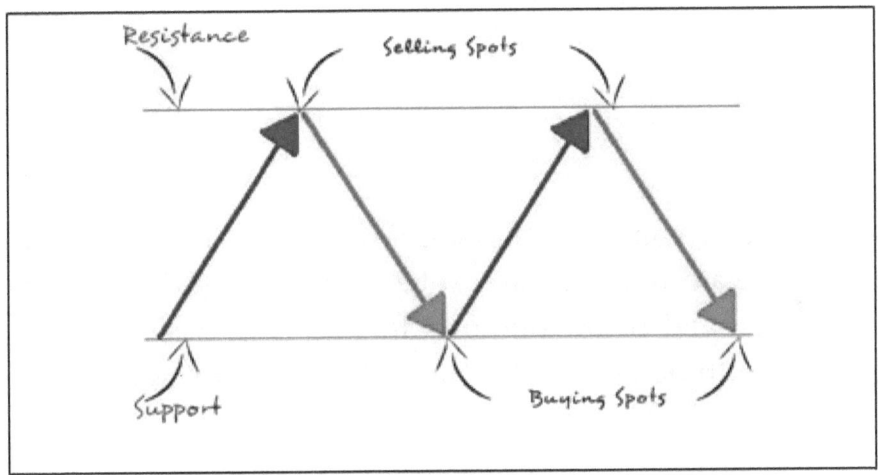

To help you confirm your entry and exit signals, you could use a momentum indicator such as the RSI, CCI or stochastics. Once the indicator signals overbought, you can look to short the market. At the same time, you can look to close out any open long position you might have.

When the indicator signals oversold, you can look to place a buy order or seek to cover any open short position you might have. The chart below best illustrates my point.

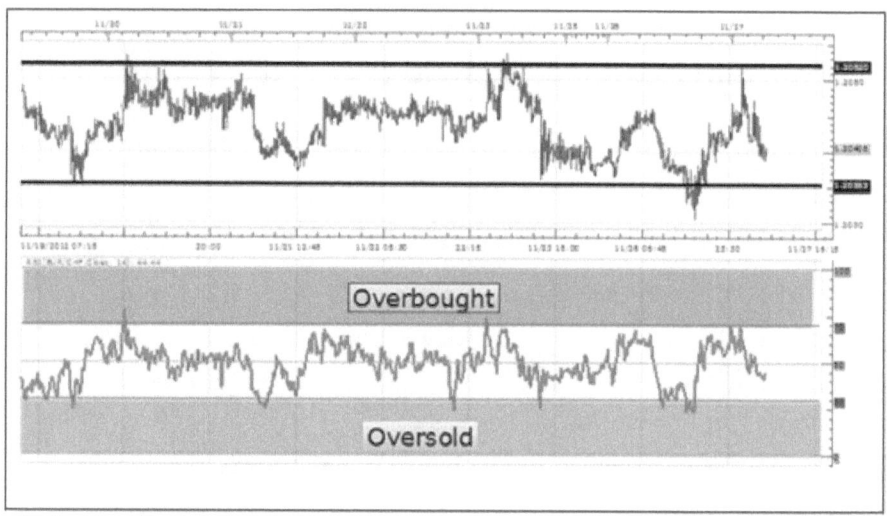

And when it comes to the stop-loss orders, common sense should dictate that they are to be placed above the highs for the shorts, and below the lows for the long positions. Take profits are to be placed at or near the support and resistance lines.

Trading a narrow-ranging market

The next type of sideways market setup is that of a narrow-range market (also called a consolidation). Here, the prices always seem to be stuck within a narrow range. Fundamentally, this could indicate indecision amongst market participants.

Most of the time, this happens when traders are anxious about a particular news event that could rock the prices in the market. So they lie quietly in wait for the outcome. When the news comes out, the market either rallies or falls sharply. This is always called a breakout. A good breakout offers a tremendous opportunity for profit.

So to begin, you need to be able to spot such a setup. This chart below shows a good example of a market in a consolidation phase. The next thing you do is draw horizontal lines marking the levels of support and resistance as shown. This helps you identify the levels at which you will need to make decisions on whether to buy or sell.

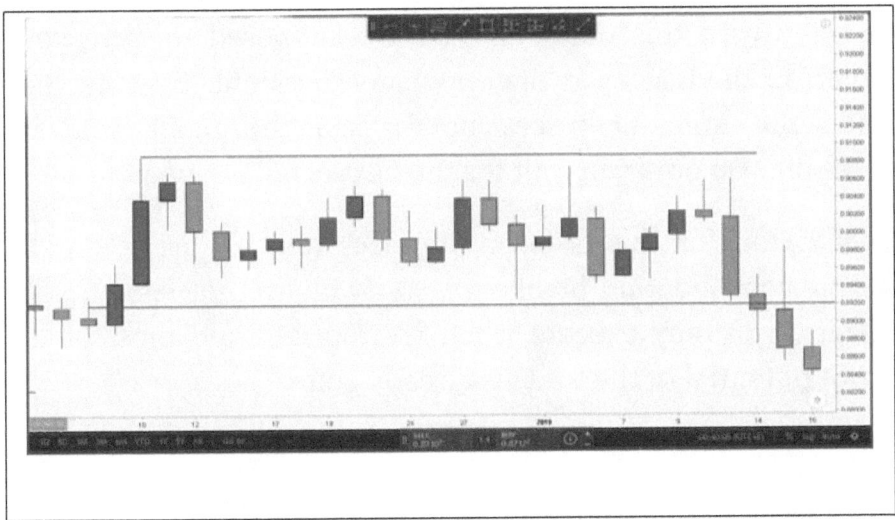

The idea is to exploit a breakout situation such as the one illustrated by this diagram.

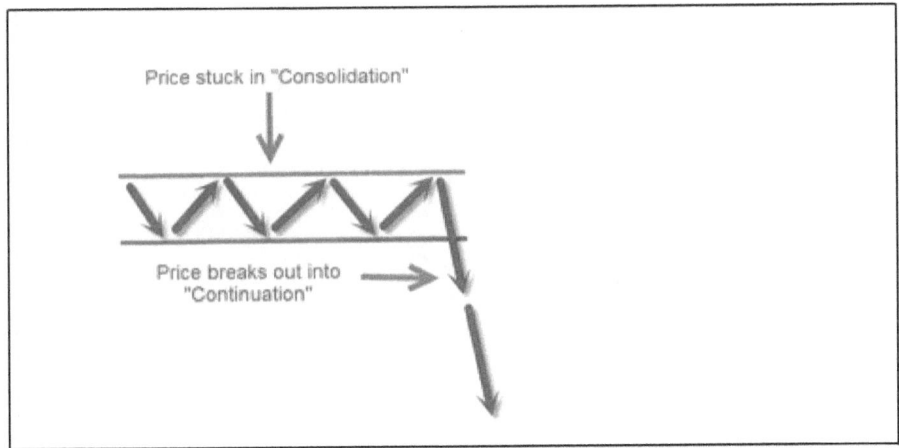

Please note that this doesn't mean that prices always break downwards. This is just one of the two scenarios that could occur. Prices could break upwards or downwards. You should be prepared for both.

If prices break upwards, you go long; if they break downwards, you go short. It is important to keep in mind that you are not to delay with this decision. You are supposed to have your finger on the trigger at the opportune moment. Execute your trade the moment prices break past the point you are watching. Do not even wait for the next candle to open.

The reason for this is because prices tend to break rapidly during consolidation breakouts, so if you are not fast on your fingers, you may execute when it's too late and most of the profit potential of the trade is already gone.

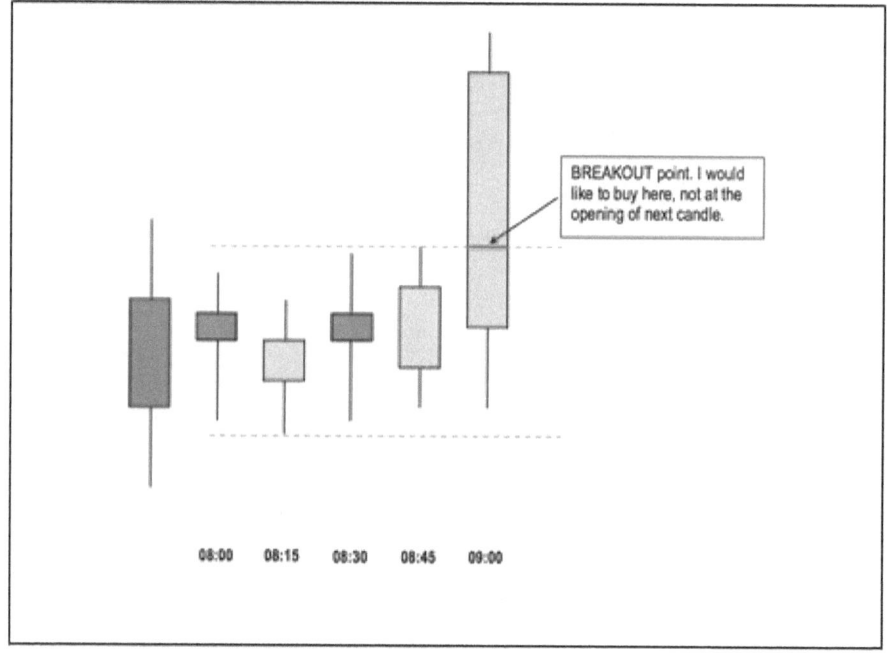

Also, executing when it is too late places you at a high risk of getting whipsawed. You get whipsawed when prices move rapidly in one direction only to suddenly reverse, taking you out of a trade incurring significant losses. So trading breakouts requires a degree of finesse. But if you are alert, very little can go wrong.

The stop-loss order for going long is to be placed below the consolidation. Conversely, stop for a short is to be placed above the consolidation. The take-profits are to be placed at a distance that is equal to twice the width of the consolidation pattern.

If you need confirmation to add value to your decision, you can use an indicator such as the "volume." When trading volume is high, the bars become long and when the trading is light, the bars are short. You can use this information to add weight to your strategy as shown in this chart.

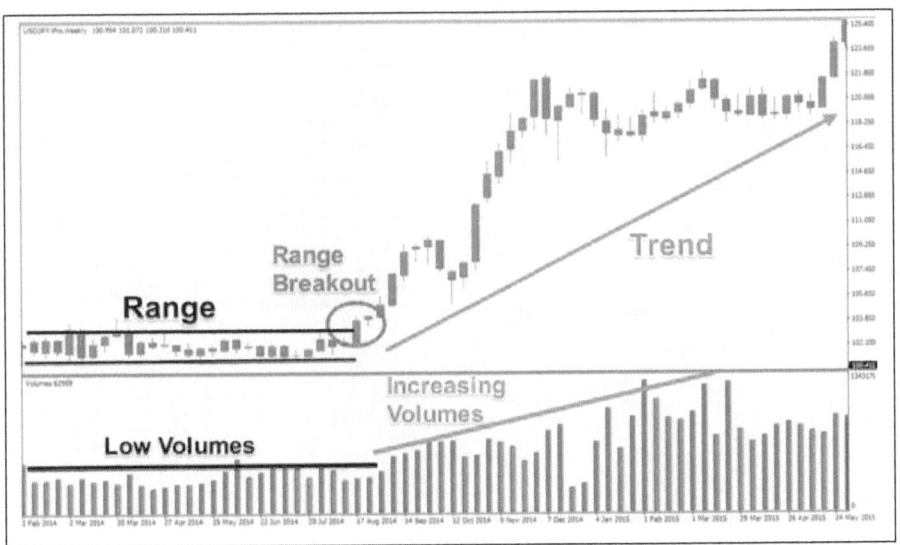

This marks the conclusion of our discussion on trading strategies. It is my hope that you are now better equipped to enter the stock market and, if presented with the right situations, execute some trades.

Let us move on to looking at how you can make investment decisions using fundamental analysis.

Fundamental Analysis - How To Make Money Slowly But Safely

Fundamental analysis is the preferred method of arriving at investment decisions for investors- people who consider themselves to be more conservative when it comes to money as compared to traders.

If you consider yourself to be a conservative person, or simply can't seem to find the time to dedicate to trading, then you will find this part of the book very valuable indeed.

We are going to look at one very effective method of investing that uses fundamental analysis – value investing. If done well and given enough time, this investment strategy can pay off in spades.

Let's look at how you can use it.

Value Investing

Value investing is the name given to the strategy that helps you identify value stocks. If you can recall from our earlier discussion, value stocks are stocks that you buy simply because you believe they are valuable.

But how exactly do you find such stocks? That is what we aim to cover.

It involves following through a number of steps, all of which ensure that the stocks you select fit a very specific criteria. Let us look at what those steps are.

Step 1: Start with companies that have a high credit rating

The first step starts with finding companies that are credit worthy. A stock cannot be a good buy if the company that issues it cannot pay its debts or is headed for bankruptcy. The stock market is full of stories about companies that went on a reckless borrowing spree and poorly allocated those funds. Such companies eventually went bust and the situation didn't work out favorably for investors.

So, you want to avoid companies like that by choosing companies that show enough promise of handling their debts. How do you find companies that fit such a criteria? I am glad you asked.

You simply consult the rating scores of companies from credit rating institutions like Standards and Poor's and Moody's. These are organizations that are established with the sole purpose of doing a background check on a company to determine its credit worthiness.

You won't have to pay a dime to acquire their data since they are paid by the actual companies to do this kind of work. Companies find that it is in their best interest to pay these institutions because they want people to know about them so that they can invest in them. It's like marketing to some extent.

Benjamin Graham – the man who developed the idea of value investing – recommends data from Standards and Poor's. And according to them, here is the scale that denotes the rating a company receives after evaluation.

Letter Grade	Grade	Capacity to Repay
AAA	Investment	Extremely strong
AA+, AA, AA-	Investment	Very strong
A+, A, A-	Investment	Strong
BBB+, BBB, BBB-	Investment	Adequate
BB+, BB	Speculative	Faces major future uncertainties
B	Speculative	Faces major uncertainties
CCC	Speculative	Currently vulnerable
CC	Speculative	Currently highly vulnerable
C	Speculative	Has filed bankruptcy petition
D	Speculative	In default

Therefore, it is best if you picked companies that have a credit score of B or better. Any company with a rating that is less than that is to be disregarded. So go ahead and compile a list of companies that fit this criteria. You will have to perform some elimination as we move on.

Step 2: Evaluate the total debt to current assets ratio

Your next task is to determine the debt to income ratio of the companies that you have chosen.

This ratio determines the total amount of debt a company has relative to its current assets. You get this ratio by dividing a company's total liabilities by its total assets.

This number seeks to establish, exactly how heavily leveraged a company's assets are. If you are wondering, leveraging is simply borrowing to invest. If you borrow money to buy a house – as is the case with mortgage financing – you are leveraging.

A highly leveraged company is a huge risk, so you want to be keen on this statistic as much as possible. Investing in companies with a low debt load is critical to your success.

According to the rules of value investing, you should eliminate all companies in your list and remain with those that have a ratio that is either 1.10 or less. Fortunately for you, you won't have to do all the legwork of getting this number. You will find it in the data you receive from Standards and Poor's.

Step 3: Determine the current ratio

Another important thing to consider is the ability of the company to pay its short term debts. Short-term debts in this case refer to debts that are payable within one year. Usually, a company needs to use its current assets (such as cash) to fulfill such obligations. If a company can do that, then it is a good candidate. And a current ratio establishes this fact.

You arrive at the current ratio by dividing current assets by current liabilities. Benjamin Graham recommends selecting companies with a current ratio of 1.50 or better. You won't have to worry about getting this number because plenty of investment services have calculated it for you – your broker included.

Step 4: Look at the earnings per share growth

The growth of a company's earnings per share is also very important. By definition, earning per share growth refers to how much the earning per share have grown over the last 12 months.

This number depicts how much a company has grown in profitability, which is also very important to you as a value investor. It is recommended that you only focus on companies whose earnings per share has shown growth over the last 5 years. If there is a deficit, eliminate those companies from your list.

Step 5: Evaluate the price to earnings (P/E) ratio

You also want to keep an eye on the price to earnings ratio. It is determined by dividing the price per share by the earnings per share of a company. This ratio is also called the earnings multiple or the price multiple.

It is a way of determining a company's value by establishing how much you as an investor would need to pay to earn $1 from company's earnings. You are advised not to overpay when purchasing a company's stock. As a matter of fact, you are required to seek bargains when shopping for stocks.

So, with regard to this, it is important that you stay away from companies with a very high price to earnings ratio. Such companies are probably high growth companies that are trading at a price that reflects the euphoria of speculative investors, more than the intrinsic value of the company.

So, select companies with a P/E ratio that is at least 9.0 or less.

Step 6: Check the price to book value (P/BV)

The P/E ratio we have just discussed may be a great way of valuing a company, but it isn't good enough. Sometimes the

P/E ratio can be misleading. Therefore, double-checking your findings with the price to book value (otherwise called market to book value) is vital.

This ratio is determined by dividing the stock's market price per share by the book value per share. You do this because the book value of a stock is often a more realistic valuation of a stock. This value can be determined from looking at a company's balance sheet.

It is recommended that you purchase stocks that have a price to book value that is less than 1.20. Doing this makes sure that you will invest in companies whose price is either below or close to their book value. This is ideal, because the essence of value investing is picking high value stocks whose price is more likely to go up in the future.

Step 7: Ensure the company issues dividends

The last thing you want to ensure is that the company you invest in issues dividends. Dividends are the portion of a company's profits that are paid off to investors periodically.

Investing in a company that issues dividends is important because you get to earn some return on your investment as you patiently wait for your investment to realize your most important objective – which could mean waiting for years.

If you follow these simple steps, you will hardly select stocks that will result in a poor return on investment. And you will have successfully put the value investing strategy to work.

Other Ways Of Earning Slow But Stable Returns On Investment

Even though value investing is a solid way of making slowly and safely in the stock market, some people may not feel comfortable working with it. You may find out that you don't trust yourself enough to do things on your own.

If that is the case, don't fret. There are some easier and more straightforward ways of making money in the stock market.

Let us look at some of them.

i)   *Mutual funds*

One way you can easily invest in the stock market is by investing in a mutual fund.

A mutual fund is a company that aims to create a pool of funds, often from the public. This money is then used to purchase different types of securities, effectively building up a diversified portfolio. For instance, you can find a mutual fund that has invested in different types of stocks, bonds, commodities, real estate or a mixture of all of them.

When you buy a mutual fund, you are purchasing a share of that company and therefore own a piece of its portfolio. It's a good way to invest in a diversified portfolio without having to go through the trouble of creating one.

This is a good thing if you are afraid of building your own portfolio, because mutual funds are managed by professional fund managers who have the necessary investment expertise.

So buying a mutual fund is a way of seeking their services cheaply.

It's also cheaper than building your own portfolio because you are building a diversified portfolio in one fell swoop, instead of purchasing individual assets by yourself, which can accumulate significant brokerage transaction costs and commissions.

Some good mutual funds you can buy include:

- Mirae Asset Large Cap fund

- Axis Bluechip Fund

- SBI Bluechip Fund

- Axis Focused Fund

- L&T India Value Fund

One thing to keep in mind is that just like a company's shares, you can sell them at any point if you decide to. They also pay out earnings from the investments to shareholders in the form of distributions.

ii)   Index funds

Index funds are another way of easily investing in the stock market. These are special mutual funds that are designed to invest in the stock market in a more passive way. By passive, I mean the managers of index funds put in little effort in researching which assets to invest in.

What index funds do is that they attempt to track or mimic the performance of an index – for instance the S&P 500. To do this, they build an investment portfolio that consists of stocks belonging to that particular index. That way, when the performance of that index rises in value, the portfolio rises in value to and vice versa.

Index funds operate on the premise that overall, buying and holding an investment works better than most investment strategies. So this is what they do more than anything else.

Because the managers rarely spend efforts in researching investment opportunities, they tend to charge lower management fees. So, if you are an investor who believes in the power of buying and holding an investment, you may want to purchase an index fund.

When you do so, you will have built a diversified stock portfolio more cheaply and with less stress.

Some good Index funds to buy include:

- Schwab S&P 500 Index Fund

- Fidelity Zero Large Cap Index

- Vanguard 500 Index Fund Investor Shares

- Fidelity 500 Index Fund

- T. Rowe Equity Index Fund

iii) Exchange-traded funds

Lastly, you have the option of investing in Exchange-Traded Funds (or ETFs).

These take the whole idea of funds to another whole level. Just like mutual funds and index funds, they can be made up of different types of assets – from stocks, to bonds, to indexes and the like. The chief difference that makes them unique is that they can be traded at an exchange at any given time provided the markets are open.

This property is what gives them that name. You see, the thing with mutual funds and index funds is that they can only be traded once per day at the end of a trading day, after the markets are closed. ETFs are far more flexible. However, the rest of the features are pretty much the same.

You can either choose to purchase an actively managed ETF or a passively managed ETF. An actively managed ETF may earn a higher return on investment but you will also have to part with more cash in the form of management fees. Passively managed ETFs only seek to track the performance of a certain basket of securities through buying and holding.

Some good ETFs to buy are:

- Vanguard Total Stock Market ETF

- Schwab U.S Small Cap ETF

- Vanguard High-Dividend Yield ETF

- Global X SuperDividend ETF

- Shares Core S&P Mid-Cap ETF

There you have it – some of the easiest and hassle-free ways of breaking into the stock market. You needn't be an expert to take advantage of these opportunities. You simply find one that has a good track record and buy it then you watch after it from time to time to see how it performs.

Which Strategy Is Best For You? A Risk Assessment Quiz

If you are having a hard time determining which investment strategy is best for you, you are not alone. Many people are in the same situation you are in – they know about the various options that they have but can't quite figure out which one they should go for.

This section deals with helping you self-examine yourself so that you decide which option is more appropriate for you. It involves asking yourself a few basic questions, nothing complicated.

Let's begin.

Question 1: How much time can you allocate to managing your investment?

In other words, how busy are you? How much free time do you get from work? If you are the busy person who has to work upwards of 12 hours per day and still has to go home to his or her family, then you are probably very busy.

In that case, it would be a really bad idea to pick an investment strategy like trading. Researching value stocks and buying mutual funds, index funds or ETFs could be your best play.

Christopher Vale, the Senior Vice President who manages Products and Solutions at Merrill Edge says:

"If you feel that you don't have the time or temperament to monitor your portfolio balances so that they stay true to your original target allocations, you could choose fund types that take on some of that work."

Question 2: How comfortable are you with making investment decisions

It is natural to feel that despite being well informed about matters concerning investment, you cannot trust yourself with such important decisions. If that is truly how you feel, then you are better off leaving such decisions to professionals who can handle them for you. So purchasing mutual funds or index funds may be your best option.

That is also what John Manetta - the Senior Portfolio manager at Merrill Lynch – advises. He says:

> *"Ask yourself if you are comfortable in the role of sole decision maker, because your results will largely rely on your choices."*

Question 3: How experienced are you when it comes to matters concerning investments?

Your level of experience matters a lot, especially when it comes to matters concerning investments. If you are less experienced, you may want to try out strategies with a lower risk profile first. Then as you become more acquainted with the investment world, you could graduate to more advanced investment strategies that involve more work and higher risk.

So, for instance, you could start with purchasing funds first. Later on, you could try purchasing some good value stocks. Then later on, you could graduate to trading a small portion of your investment portfolio and maybe increase that amount as you become more successful at it.

Question 4: How much of a risk taker are you?

We all have to take on some risk when we participate in the financial markets. There's just no way around that simple fact. Nevertheless, we are not the same when it comes to the level of risk we can tolerate. So ask yourself, "What is my risk tolerance level? Is it low, medium, or high?"

Knowing where you fall on that scale can help you make the right decision. For instance, if you consider yourself a high risk taker, then trading is probably a good choice for you. If you are a medium risk taker, value investing is probably a good idea. Then, if you are a low risk taker, you may find that purchasing funds is the best way to go.

You know yourself better, so be your own judge.

Question 5: How much time do you have?

You should also pick your strategy keeping in mind the amount of time you have. As a general rule, you shouldn't go for investments such as purchasing funds and value investing if you fear that you only have a few years to live – unless you plan on leaving that investment to your children and grandchildren.

But if you are young and have anywhere between 20 years to 30 years or more ahead of you, by all means go for it. But if you have little time on earth and would like to maximize the use of your time, money and other resources, then taking on a venture of higher risk like trading would be more appropriate.

Question 6: What is your primary goal in investing?

The reasons for investing are not universal. Of course, we all invest to make money but the reasons for making that money are diverse. Some people do it to balance the risk in their portfolio. Some people invest to hedge against the poor performance of other assets. You may invest as an insurance policy should a bad economic event occur. You may be investing so that you buy a car in five years. Many people may invest so that they have enough money for their old age.

Whatever your reasons are, you must pick a strategy that aligns with your goals. So go ahead and ask yourself what your main reason for investing is and pick accordingly.

I hope these few questions go a long way in helping you arrive at the right decision regarding which strategy to pick. It's all a matter of self-assessment. Let's move on past this and discuss how you can actually get into the game.

Getting Into The Game

You are sufficiently informed on strategy. The next important thing is getting into the game. This part of the book will guide you through that. We will begin by looking at various investment accounts that you should know of. Then from there, we will look at how you can open a brokerage account and then proceed to make your first investment.

Then we will look at a few basics of managing risk:

Types Of Investment Accounts

There are different types of accounts where you can put money that is meant for investment purposes. But they vary in terms of features.

Let us look at each one in turn.

1. Individual Retirement Accounts

The first type of investment account is an Individual Retirement Account (or an IRA). This is a type of investment account that is better suited for you if you are investing for retirement purposes. They allow you to invest in a wide variety of financial assets such as stocks, commodities, bonds and so on.

The main benefit of working with this kind of account is that you get tax benefits. You are allowed to defer your taxes to the time when you decide to sell the assets and get your money out of the account. There are however rules defining how much money you can put into the account per year and when you can get the funds out of the account.

There are different types of Individual Retirement Accounts.

They include:

o   Roth IRAs

o   Traditional IRAs

o   SEP IRAs

o   Simple IRAs

I am not going to go deep into the details of these accounts, because these are not the type of accounts that you will mostly deal with - unless you are specifically investing for retirement. You can read more about them from Investopedia.

2. *Employer Sponsored Accounts*

You also have investment accounts that are sponsored by employers. Like IRAs, these accounts are meant for investing retirement money.

The also offer some tax advantages. In addition to that, depending on your employer, he or she can offer to match your monthly contributions. Your employer doing this is the equivalent of you receiving free money.

If you get such a chance, you should take it.

Types of Employer Sponsored Accounts include:

o   Traditional 401 (k)s

o   Roth 401 (k)s

o   Traditional retirement plans

- 403 (b)s

- 457s

3. Taxable Brokerage accounts

Lastly, we have taxable brokerage accounts. These are the accounts that you will mostly work with because they allow for utmost flexibility. There also no limit to which type of assets you can invest in.

The only problem is that capital gains – those which you get from your stocks appreciating in price – are taxed. But, you have the freedom of operating with these accounts as you wish. The two types of taxable brokerage accounts that exist are:

- Individual Taxable Brokerage accounts – these are limited to one person only

- Joint taxable brokerage accounts – these allow two or more people to sign on it.

Opening A Brokerage Account

Opening a brokerage account is simple. You simply identify a broker with a good reputation and you fill an online form asking you for some basic identity information. You fill it and wait for account verification. Once your account is verified, you can deposit your investment capital and start purchasing some stocks.

There are so many good brokers out there. The industry is highly competitive and you won't encounter any shortage of them.

Here are some that I personally recommend.

- Fidelity Investments

- TD Ameritrade

- TradeStation

- Charles Schwabb

- Interactive brokers

- Robinhood

- ETrade

- Ally Invest

- Merrill Edge

Making Your First Investment

After opening your brokerage account, you will need to deposit money to that account. Your broker will have detailed instructions on how you can do that. After doing that, your next step is to make your first investment.

In market terms, this is called placing an order

It is vital that you know that there are different types of orders in the financial markets, all designed for different types of purposes.

In this case I will mention the two that you need to know of:

i)   *Market orders*

Market orders are what you work with when you are investing for the long-term. For instance, when you are purchasing value stocks, or a mutual fund, this is the type of order you will work with. This is because market prices can fluctuate so you need to sit them out.

ii)   *Limit orders*

Limit orders, on the other hand, are designed for traders. This is because traders need to implement very strict risk management strategies to their practices. For instance, stop-loss orders and take-profit orders that we talked about when discussing trading strategies are examples of limit orders.

You can place these orders through the trading software that your broker issues you after you open your account with them.

The good thing with placing orders on the market is that you can seek the assistance of your broker in case you are having any problems. Good brokers offer great customer service and helping you execute your market orders is part of their job description. So you shouldn't worry about getting stuck with this step.

Managing Your Money – Learning How To Limit Your Losses

Risk management is critical when you are investing your money. There is always the risk of losing money when you invest. Therefore, you need to protect your investment the best way you can to avoid losing all of your investment capital.

Risk management is a deep subject so I will talk about two main ways of managing risk that you need to know of.

i) *The 2% rule of money management*

This rule is better suited for traders. The rule is this: for any given trade, you are not supposed to risk more than 2% of the total value of your investable assets. In reality, you should keep that number to at least 1%. You need to risk lesser than that especially if you are a scalper who executes several transactions per day.

In other words, if you have $100,000 in investment capital, you are supposed to risk either $2,000 per trade or less.

If you risk only such portions, you can lose on a lot of your trades and still retain a huge portion of your capital. That way, if you happen to enter a winning streak, you can still make a profit. But even more important, you will have protected your investment capital. This kind of risk management is what makes trading work, despite involving such high risks.

ii) *Diversification*

Another way you can limit your risk is by diversifying the assets that you hold in your portfolio.

Diversification is a theory that was invented by Harry Markowitz. The idea is that by spreading your investment capital across various unrelated assets, you reduce the overall risk. This happens because you hedge each asset against the other. If one stock investment starts performing poorly, another one may start gaining value. Therefore, the risk of losing money in one asset is countered with again in another.

Therefore, if you are investing in the stock market, make sure that you do not put all your money in one stock. Try and spread it over several different types of stock. If you are unsure on how you can do that, then you can purchase ETFs, mutual funds or index funds. Those instruments are developed by professionals who have a firm grasp of the concept.

Closing thoughts

At this point, you are much more informed, and can make mush wiser investment decisions in the stock market. But before you do that, let's go over some important things you should keep in mind, so that you operate more safely in the marketplace.

Why Investors And Traders Lose Money - 10 Huge Trading Mistakes

Traders lose money most of the time due to lack of discipline. And if you understand what the common triggers of trader indiscipline are, you will be in a much better position to avoid destroying yourself as a trader.

Let us look at what some of those triggers are and how you can avoid them.

1. Allowing your emotions to cloud your judgment

The first mistake that you shouldn't make as a trader is getting your emotions involved in your trading. Remember, in trading there is always the risk of losing your money. Also, there is the possibility of getting a huge payoff when a trade works out. And where money is involved like this, it is possible to get emotional.

As a trader, you should do your best to keep your emotions out of your trading. You should try and come up with various mental strategies of keeping your emotions in control as you trade.

One good strategy is that of looking at trading as a game. Try not to look at the entire trading activity as a money-making venture. Try and imagine that your winnings and losses are points in a game. If you look at trading this way, you not only keep emotions from your trading, it also becomes more fun.

2. Failing to follow your plan

Another mistake you can make in trading is that of trading without a plan. The thing is, trading is a game of chance. You are merely playing the odds. The only way you can beat the game is by creating a plan – which means coming up with a strategy - and following that plan.

Going against that plan is a recipe for disaster. This is one of the main reasons why traders fail. When you fail to stick to your plan, you insert random variables to your trading regime, which make it that much harder to make money. So you must do your best and follow that plan.

3. Taking on too much risk per trade

Taking on too much risk is another reason why traders may lose money. As a trader, you may look at a trade and feel that your chances are good. This is when you may fall for making the mistake of betting too much on such a trade.

Never do this.

You can never guarantee that any trade will work out, no matter how good it looks. You may get lucky and the risk works out, but making that mistake once makes it more likely that you will repeat it in the future. And the truth is, you never get lucky every time.

And when that happens, you could lose a lot of capital that makes it hard for you to ever recover. This is one of those mistakes that destroy the career of many traders with great potential. So steer clear of it.

4. Adding to a losing position

It is said that most people are less tolerant of risk when a trade is going in their favor and become more tolerant of risk when things are going wrong. What this means is that when you are losing money on a bad trade, you are more likely to tolerate that loss with the hopes that your luck will eventually turn around.

This makes you commit one of the cardinal sins in trading, moving your stop-loss order. The problem is when you start moving that stop, you can never be sure how far the market is going to keep going against you. You may find yourself raising that stop even more, and before you know it, you will have lost plenty.

So what do you instead? Simply do this; when you place a stop-loss order on the market, stick to it. It is much better to take that small loss and move on. As long as you limited your risk to less than 2%, you should be fine. Write off that loss from your mind and keep looking for another opportunity.

And when you encounter a winning trade, try to ride it as much as you can by trailing both your stop as well as the take-profit order. There is a golden rule in trading that says: cut your losses short and let your profits run. Follow it.

5. Getting euphoric

This is another trap that begets many traders.

As you trade and keep following the rules of your system, inevitably, you will start to taste some success. You may even come across, what is known in the industry as a winning streak. A big mistake you can make is that of becoming overconfident of your abilities as a trader.

This cockiness can make you commit some of the biggest mistakes in trading that could end up ruining you both as a trader and a person – such as risking too much on a trade. So, the best thing you can do is remember that trading is risky and that winning streaks always come to an end. And as long as you follow your plan, you should be confident that you will be successful in the long-term.

6. *Allowing yourself to get swayed by the news*

Keeping your head in the game and trusting your plan is also one of the biggest challenges you will ever face as a trader or investor. This is especially true in this information age.

Once you are in a position - say in a stock such as Apple Inc. – you may get some news that make you doubt your position and want to change your mind. Never fall for this trap. Always remember that trading is all about religiously following a plan, not matter what the circumstances may be.

Never compromise on anything. When you break a rule and listen to outside influences, you stop operating systematically and you introduce random variables to your system and this has the ability of destroying your chances of maintaining consistent success.

7. *Not using an appropriate risk-reward ratios*

This one is a common one. Remember, earlier, I pointed out that your risk reward ratio should be at least 1:2. Never break that rule, because it is this rule that helps you make more money than you lose. When you follow this rule consistently, you make it more likely that you will win in the long run, even though you may run into many losers.

To illustrate, let's imagine that after executing 10 trades, only four worked out and six failed. And let's imagine that you kept your risk consistent at $100 per trade. If you run the number, you will find that you still come out a winner on balance.

Take a look:

6 losers @ $100

6 losers X 100   = $600

4 winners @ $200

4 winners X $200   = $800

Subtract the losers from the winners

$800 - $600   = $200

So, as you can see, according to this basic math, you can still win even though you may have lost more than 50% of the time. This is the magic that can keep you successful as a trader for a long time despite the odds being stacked against you.

8. Failing to review your performance

As a trader, you need to periodically review your performance. This is necessary so that you know whether what you are doing is working. It also helps you establish whether you are disciplined enough to follow a systematic plan.

So, in order for you to ensure that you stay on track, you need to keep a trading journal. This is a journal like any other only that it is used to keep a record of all your trades. You need to do this so that you have easy access to what you have been doing.

It also keeps you in line because you will always remember that you have to record each and every trade. This will make you think twice before making a bad trade that goes against your rules.

Once you have a journal like this, you can choose to do your own assessment on your own timeframe. Ideally, you should do it every month but doing it once every two weeks is also a good idea. During this exercise, go over you results and examine each trade and see where you may have gone wrong.

9. *Trading with a bad broker*

Another fatal mistake you may make is that of trading with a bad broker. Never compromise on this. You especially need to pay attention to the commissions and fees you get charged.

You see, profit margins in trading are very tight. High commissions can eat away at your gains and make it hard for you to operate profitable. The best way to avoid this problem is to select a reputable broker. When in doubt about your ability to select one, simply pick one from the list I gave you earlier.

Those are brokers who have a long history of commendable service to investors. They have a solid reputation and that isn't likely to change any time soon because that is what gives them a competitive advantage in this industry. You would be wise to work with them.

10. *Inconsistent position sizes*

Another mistake is that of failing to keep your position size consistent. If you want the trading math to work in your favor, you must try your best to keep your risk consistent.

So, for instance, if you decide to trade at $100 per trade, stay with that decision and never change it. Don't lower it to say $90 or ramp it up to $200. That will make it hard for you to keep your performance consistent. It will also make it hard to determine what works and what doesn't, especially when you are conducting periodic reviews.

If you try and avoid these few trading mistakes, you will find that your trading performance will become much better and you will become more consistent with your profits. Your life as trader will even become easier.

Conclusion

We have finally reached the final part of this book. I must admit that it has been a long time coming. It is my hope that you have received much value from this book.

My only ask is that you put this information to practice. Knowledge isn't power unless you do something about applying it.

All in all, I want to thank you for your support by purchasing this book. Your contribution goes a long way in making sure that I and my associates will keep bringing more useful products like these to the market to serve people like you.

I wish you great success in your investment aspirations. And may God bless you abundantly. I hope to meet you once again in a similar book like this one.